The accounts in this book are true, but to protect the victims, the innocent, and even the guilty, most names have been changed.

Books by Wanjiru Warama

Unexpected America

Entangled in America

YEARS of SHAME

YEARS of SHAME

FGM SURVIVOR & OTHER TRUE STORIES

Wanjiru Warama

Athomi Books

California, United States of America

YEARS of SHAME

wanjiruwarama.com

wanjiru.warama@gmail.com

Published September 2018

United States of America

First Edition

ISBN: 978-0998051352

Published by Athomi Books

8064 Allison Avenue, #684, La Mesa, California, CA 91942

United States of America

This book is dedicated to every girl or woman who has no say or control over her own body

TABLE OF CONTENTS

PART ONE

PART TWO

PART THREE

PART FOUR

PART FIVE

PART ONE

The Women's Factory

Chapter One

It's Only a Girl

Njana rushed from her Nairobi office, thankful her boss had allowed her to leave early. Her bag dangled at her side, the strap slung over her shoulder. She was not looking forward to the experience; she hated to have to visit the "women's factory" and hoped it would be her first and last time.

Since her morning-break, when she received a phone call from her brother, Menya, and even as she walked to the parking lot, she tried but failed to forget the "women's factory." The term conjured chaotic images of screaming babies popping out of a human shoot, bumping along the sides of a conveyor belt.

*****

As Njana walked to the parking lot, she felt grateful she did not have to ride in one of those *matatu* vans that drivers jammed passengers into as if they were bales of coffee sacks headed to the Kenya Cooperative Coffee Factory, instead of humans headed to work or home.

"Let him get in!" a conductor would say. Or "Let her get in!" Always room for one more as long as there was an opening to squeeze into and hang onto the overhead grab bar, or get sandwiched in between anxious strange bodies.

Njana reached the spot where she had parked her car in the morning, opened the driver's door of her white Toyota Corolla, and sat in the driver's seat. Before she turned on the engine, she let her eyes wander around the grey interior. She did this routine whenever the urge hit, a satisfied reminder that she now owned a car. An achievement so lofty she had never imagined it until three years earlier, the time she drove her boyfriend's old grey VW beetle for 120 miles alone without a license. Her parents and their neighbors had treated her with deference, the pride of the village. That was when she started thinking, maybe I could own a car.

Njana reminded herself to focus. She started the car and headed to Pumwani Maternity Hospital, a relic of the British colonial administration, which they had built for African expectant mothers.

In the seventies and the eighties, and perhaps beyond, that was where they still took every pregnant low-income woman in Nairobi who winced and stretched and said, "It's time!" even if it took her baby another day to venture into the world.

The local government, or whoever was responsible for birthing wards for low-income families, lagged behind in upgrading the earlier colonial setup of barely functional hospitals for the Africans.

*****

A woman whose husband owned a stash of shillings, or held a senior post in government, or the private business sector, went to a maternity where they babied the mother along with her newborn. Such a woman went to Nairobi Hospital or Kenyatta Hospital Maternity Ward, both formerly designated for Europeans before Kenya's independence, or the Agha Khan Hospital, previously set aside for Indians.

Menya, Njana's brother, was like the majority of Nairobi residents. He did not have enough shillings, influence, or fringe benefits from his employer to get his wife pampered.

Chapter Two

Pumwani Maternity Hospital

At Pumwani Maternity, Njana asked to see her sister-in-law. The receptionist checked in a register at her desk. "There is no Njoki Menya listed here," she said.

"How could that be?" Njana asked. "My brother said his wife is here."

"Well, he was mistaken."

"Mistaken? He talked to me."

"Does she have another name?"

"No."

"As I said, there is nobody by that name on this list."

"He brought her last night."

"You are welcome to check for yourself," the receptionist said, "That's the waiting room." She pointed straight ahead to a corridor in need of a fresh coat of paint.

The so-called waiting room could have depressed even a slum-dweller. It was filled with stressed, expectant mothers. They sat on benches waiting and hoping for a free bed at the labor ward before their little ones popped out. Occasionally, a nurse came into the room, her eyes alert, to identify any mother whose baby could not wait to emerge. Some women wiggled, eyes squeezed shut to stifle the pain without compromising their dignity.

Mothers still able to carry on a conversation did not let their fidgety neighbors deter them. They recycled stories of previous incidents they had heard of. One was that a month did not go by without a baby forcing its way out, right there in the waiting room, and bawling to its vocal cords capacity without a tear to show for the effort. The other mothers would gawk and think, oh Lord, please let it not happen to me.

*****

After Njana got her bearings at the large waiting room, she spotted the apparent head midwife. Although the woman wore a uniform similar to a nurse's, she had stripes sewn on her white cap, designating a higher rank. At about five-eight with a proportionate frame, she wore an air of authority, standing by the corridor toward the labor ward, holding a clipboard on which she made check marks, to ensure the system worked smoothly despite the congestion.

Njana approached the midwife when she seemed to have a minute to spare. "I'm looking for Njoki Menya."

"You need to check at the reception."

"I've just come from there," Njana said. "They said I check here."

"If the reception doesn't have her name," the midwife said, "I'm afraid she's not here."

"How can that be?" Njana said. "My brother brought her last night. She gave birth today."

"I have names of new mothers right here," the midwife said, her finger going down the list on the clipboard. "Her name is not listed," she said, impatience in her voice, exhaustion on her shiny face.

"I'll wait until somebody can locate her," Njana said, walked the few steps back into the waiting room, and stood by the wall. She was out of the way but near enough to watch women contort their faces or hear them hiss through clenched teeth, or grunt from intermittent labor pangs and for the midwife to notice her.

*****

Njana waited and waited, shifting her weight from one leg to the other or leaning against the wall. No wonder those men referred to the hospital as "The Women's Factory," she thought.

She had learned of the term at a bar south of Tom Mboya Street in downtown Nairobi two years prior. She considered the bar a little seedy, despite the patronage of some rich men, men who clung to insecurities from their humble beginnings, the possibility of falling back into poverty not too far from their minds.

These men felt uneasy in finer establishments where patrons valued and guarded their public personas no matter what crummy lives they led in their private lives.

After work, Njana had dropped in at the bar to consult a councilman about recommending one of her relatives for employment at the Nairobi City Council. She wished the man had suggested they meet at one of those trendy cafes. But if a man of his caliber patronized the marginal place on a regular basis, and she needed a favor from him, who was she to complain about his choice?

At the bar, the councilman was well into his drinking binge for the night. He sat at a table with three other men, two of whom seemed to belong while the third seemed ill at ease. Perhaps he was just another favor-seeker.

"Bring a chair for the young lady," the councilman said, "and ask her what she wants to drink."

"I'll have Baby Cham," Njana said, a fad drink—perhaps wine—young women at the time preferred. It signified, in their minds at least, that they were modern women.

Men loathed Baby Cham—a total waste of money, vocal men with little money to spare said. Two mouthfuls and one drained the tiny bottle.

At the next table sat a group of jovial men, dressed in office attire, except one, downing glasses of Pilsner or Tusker. One of them was drinking a clear drink, possibly vodka. "It's about time you returned to the factory," the vodka man said.

"Yes, I better get going," said the casually dressed man Njana later learned was a gynecologist.

"What factory?" another man asked.

"You don't know?" the vodka man asked. "Pumwani Maternity is called 'The Women's Factory.'"

After the doctor left, the other men made smutty jokes about the factory that manufactured babies day and night. They enjoyed throaty chuckles as if the vodka man had just told them the funniest female joke of the year.

After the fun subsided, one of the men said the doctor was the most qualified at Pumwani Maternity Hospital, except that he drank too much. There were also whispers, the vodka man said, that the doctor performed too many cesarean sections even on mothers who, given more time, could have had natural deliveries.

*****

No matter how much Njana tried to distract herself, she still overheard some of the expectant mothers' conversations. One was that, after a baby arrived, one sleepover for mother and child sufficed before the staff ushered the two out the door unless there were complications. That meant Njoki would have been going home that very day instead of missing.

Finally, the midwife became tired of seeing Njana every time she, the midwife, turned around. "Go in the wards and check for yourself," she said.

Njana walked through the hallway the midwife indicated. Afraid of what she might find, she gingerly entered a room full of women, each lying down in a twin bed next to her newborn. Others lay on raggedy bedding spread on old mattresses on the floor.

Njoki was not among the women.

Njana returned to the corridor and turned to her left. In a few steps, she saw the nursery—tucked away from relatives eager to get early peeks at their new family members or possible sneaky baby-snatchers. The nursery was reserved for newborns of problem births when mothers could not take care of their infants.

Nobody stopped Njana, but she realized her mistake, backtracked, and turned the opposite direction. She was bumped twice by nurses who said, "Pardon me," as they rushed by.

Njana entered the next room. Just like the first one, it had small windows and musty air from congestion and limited oxygen. Her nostrils were hit by a stale smell, likely from body odor and birthing aftermath. Her eyes darted around the room. Sometimes she went close and bent slightly to check the faces of the women who snoozed, arms rested on their temples.

Njana got lucky in the third room. Njoki lay stretched on a twin bed with her tiny bundle next to her, swaddled in a cloth and a towel. Relieved, Njana rushed in. Njoki, alerted by the arrival, propped her head on her elbow. She looked lethargic, but managed a weak smile.

"I've been so worried," Njana said. "They didn't have your name anywhere."

"A person could die in here," Njoki said, "and it would take a day before they found out."

"Is the baby okay?"

"Hm! it's only a girl," Njoki said, frowned and clicked her tongue as she flipped the cover off the baby's head to introduce Njana.

Confused by Njoki's remark, Njana stood speechless, not knowing what to say. She had always been sensitive to the degrading way men treated or dismissed women and girls, many times with the help of other women.

Despite her mother's dismissal, the new baby was lucky to have been born in the mid-seventies, and in Nairobi. She would not have to suffer the trauma that Njana had undergone in her teen years in the backwoods of Kenya.

Chapter Three

Maternity Dramas

Njoki's demeaning of her infant daughter was not an isolated case. Women's marginalization by parents and the larger society started from birth. But after Kenya's independence from Britain on December 12, 1963, the government started and continues to make efforts to minimize the inequality between men and women.

The only time politicians dithered about passing a statute on equality, acting as if they were confused about what women wanted, was when some asserted that feminists wanted a legal way to dominate men. Or if an issue interfered with the politicians' reelection, they insulated themselves by delaying and kicking the unsettled matter forward to the next generation of lawmakers.

But, all in all, the government had made inroads. Parliament passed a law allowing women to participate in the previously men-only National Social Security Fund (NSSF). Women started contributing to their NSSF retirement accounts in 1975. By then, society had stopped frowning so much when a woman went into a profession other than teaching, nursing, or secretarial.

Other rights followed, including inheritance rights, travel rights where a wife or daughter could get her own passport instead of having her name on the father's or husband's passport, and women could hold property titles in their own names.

But the domination of women by men and some privileged women as part of the social fabric remained intact, and at best a work-in-progress.

Njana had heard women voters say, "How can I vote for a woman who wears a dress like me? What can she tell me that I don't already know?" Or "What can she do for me that I can't do for myself?"

Such self-loathing utterances stung Njana, and she sometimes personalized the women's remarks. Her mind, however, remained fuzzy on how she could fight such attitudes.

*****

Now at Pumwani Maternity, when women's burdens swirled in Njana's mind, she avoided asking the name of her new niece. It did not matter. She already knew it the minute Njoki pronounced, "It's only a girl." She and her husband had named their last daughter after Menya's sister, according to the Gikūyū tradition of alternating naming of children between the husband's and wife's families. That meant they would name the newborn Binti, after Njoki's sister because she had already named one daughter after her mother.

With both women unwilling to say more about baby Binti, Njoki wanted to talk, mostly gossip about what she had heard since she entered the Women's Factory the previous day. She scooted over a few inches and invited Njana to sit at the edge of the rickety wrought-iron twin bed.

Njana hesitated. She felt out of place, wearing business attire: a belted red dress, black two-inch pumps, her legs in nylons and her hair salon styled, with curls from nightly spongy rollers.

She looked such a contrast from the new mothers. They seemed so vulnerable and weary, with sweaty-faces, wearing tired dresses with *leso* wrappers tied at their waists, their hair braids disheveled or covered in scarves.

Njana also made efforts to overcome the confusion that lingered in her mind regarding the issue of boy versus girl children, especially now that Njoki had blatantly demeaned her newborn.

Njana's unspoken belief at that time remained: birth-of-a-girl disappointment should be reserved for couples without a male child. Njoki and Menya already had two sons; were those not enough?

Njana did not realize it then, but she was a product of the society from which she grew up in and, although parents' preference for male children assaulted her sensibilities, she was not enlightened more than Njoki.

*****

First-born daughters, however, are treated differently. New parents are happy to get any child. And if parents bring forth a line of sons, they are happy to have a daughter or two to break the monotony.

The only other time a girl child is preferred is if the mother is single, and not too advanced in years. The mother's chance of marriage does not diminish much since men do not balk at marrying a woman with a girl child.

*****

Njana brushed her indecision aside; it was not as if Njoki had asked her to sleep in that congested room. She stepped forward and sat at the corner of the twin bed, nearer to Njoki's outstretched legs. Njoki patted the bed, signaling to Njana to move closer. She inched closer, knees folded as if she sat on a low stool, her bag on the floor next to her feet.

Njoki jutted her chin toward a woman across the room and said in a low voice, "That woman's child is in the nursery."

"Is the baby all right? Njana asked.

"It's the mother."

"What's wrong with her?"

"She has fainting spells but the doctor can't find anything wrong with her. He's approved extra days for observation."

"Hmm," Njana said.

"When there is no nurse or doctor around, she talks as if there is nothing wrong with her. There is a rumor that she's faking illness so she can heal before she returns to her sex-starved husband."

"That can't be true."

"It happens," Njoki said, shifted, and propped herself to a sitting position.

Njana inched out and yielded some more inches for Njoki and the baby.

"In the next room, there is a woman who gave birth to a child who is both boy and girl," Njoki said. "What do you call that, hermaphrodite?"

"Poor woman," Njana replied.

"After the midwife told the husband, he became agitated. "He said he and his wife didn't have anybody freaky like that in their families. When the wife returned home, he said, she would have a lot of explaining to do. He left without seeing her or paying the hospital bill."

What a depressing story! Njana promised herself she would never visit Pumwani Maternity again. She had previously heard other pathetic incidents.

One story was about a man with three daughters. On learning his wife had given birth to their fourth girl, he turned around, went to a bar, drank himself silly while he lamented about his bad luck to his table mates. He awoke at the bar in the morning and went home to nurse his hangover. He fetched his wife and baby a day later.

At the time, men were still unaware that fathers determine the gender of a baby. A judgmental person might have told the disappointed husband that his squiggly tadpoles dragged their feet during the one and only sprint of their short lives.

Another story Njana had heard about was of a man who had waited in the hospital compound, machete in hand, in case his wife killed their baby. The wife's crazed birthing-labor behavior had already resulted in the death of one child.

As the story went, she had gone berserk, rolled and writhed, shouting for her mama's help because the pain would kill her. The pain spared her but killed the baby.

But this second time, the husband was determined to have a different outcome as he paced in the hospital vicinity. If the wife killed that baby, he said, he would bury mother and child together.

Worried about the two-to-a-grave threat, the midwives tied the woman onto the birthing bed for a whole day until she gave birth. Her hollers may have traumatized the baby, but they did not cause death. The husband took his wife and baby boy home, everybody happy that no one ended up in the morgue.

Commentary

Pumwani Maternity Hospital has now evolved. Such husband maternity dramas are unheard of, and those that remain have gone underground or are too subtle for people to gossip about. There is no way, however, to assess parents'—especially fathers'—private anguish when births do not come out as desired.

PART TWO

Njana's story - 1

Chapter Four

A Flicker of Hope

Njana hungered for a state of serene wellness and connection. But she continued to feel unfulfilled and out of balance. She blamed her melancholy state on a new culture. But she knew better. Although the change to a new locale had contributed to it, wholeness had eluded her for many years, even in Kenya, her country of birth, no matter what she accomplished.

Like millions of others, she had clawed through the vagaries of life:

- Broke today, money tomorrow

- Relationship here and a dry spell there
- Self-doubt, why-me malaise, confident
- Secrets, anger, shame, and hunger for wellness...

Ordinary recycled life incidents— from one generation to the next—details that Njana did not care to rehash when she ended up in the United States.

She lived in a townhome in Point Loma, San Diego, California, a settled community where she had no fear of an arm slipping around her neck from behind.

Most people would be happy to spend their entire lives in Point Loma; amenities to support good living in close proximity—the airport, the ocean, good eateries, shops, good neighbors, and downtown.

Her romantic relationship had not worked out as she had expected. She was on her own, earning a living as a secretary and working on establishing herself as a financial planner or real estate investor.

Njana had turned one bedroom into an office where she worked in the evenings and weekends, or when she had a day off. She kept the TV on as background noise in the living room.

On her way to the kitchen to get a glass of water, she turned to the TV when she heard Geraldo Rivera's voice—his shows were always lively. Before Njana learned whether it was his show or not, she froze when she heard the topic. The panel was discussing—female genital mutilation (FGM) reconstructive surgery. A flash like lightning ran through Njana, ending in a spasm in her genitalia. Her heart raced, eyes wide, determined not to miss anything.

But the segment turned out to be just a blip in the program about various women's challenges. The panel moved on to other topics before Njana caught the surgeon's name.

Was such surgery possible? she wondered. How could one get in touch with someone in the show? Without a way to know, Njana's interest subsided. Her burden retreated to where it had resided for years, deep within her.

Back at her desk, she willed the subject out of her thoughts but the incident would not fade away.

The possibility of such a surgery kept popping into her mind during the following days. To calm herself, Njana sent a letter to Dear Abby, the newspaper columnist, asking her whether she knew of a doctor who did FGM reconstructive surgery to whom she could refer her.

After Njana mailed the letter, she debated with herself whether to keep a copy. She felt ashamed to have put such an issue in writing. If she died, she thought, a friend or family member would find the letter and learn of her secret agony. She willed herself to stop the worry and buried a copy among her important papers.

Chapter Five

Rites of Passage

Before colonization, rites of passage or circumcision was a solemn event. It was the time Gikūyū teenage boys and girls transitioned from childhood to adulthood. Individuals circumcised in the same year belonged to a *rica,* an age group similar to a Boy Scout or Girl Guide troop. Every *rica* had a name. That was how the tribe kept track of their citizens' ages.

In the three to four weeks it took the new initiates to heal, they were fed a special diet of meats, spiced soups, and grains. They learned about their changing bodies, relationship with the opposite sex, hygiene, how to be responsible and accountable to each other, how to be custodians of the tribe's traditions, and finally how to defend and maintain the Gikūyū bloodline as the children of Gikūyū and Mūmbi, the Gikūyū primordial parents.

A sponsor became like a second mother or father to the initiate, worthy of great respect. The sponsor's duty was to support his or her candidate during the circumcision, the healing, and education process, and to avail herself or himself for consultation and advice even in later years. The teaching took place in separate venues—boys and girls in their respective groups.

After Kenya was conquered and occupied by the British, the indigenous people's traditions, including rites of passage, became maligned, marginalized and progressively watered down. By the 1960s, rites of passage had ceased to be a comprehensive induction stage, similar to quinceañera practiced by the Spanish-speaking communities or bar Mitzvah by the Jews.

Instead, the only aspect of the Gikũyũ rites of passage that remained was the meaningless removal of penis foreskin for boys and clitoral cutting for girls, as if cutting sexual parts of bodies put adult wisdom into teenagers' minds.

Chapter Six

Njana

Njana was born and raised in Ilaso, Nakuru County in Kenya. Ilaso was as far away as one could get from modernity. But it was better than some other godforsaken places in the country where people did not even have schools.

Her parents scratched out a living as farm workers on a British farmer's land. Her life in the village of sticks, mud, and thatched round houses was uneventful. It had no extreme variations. With little outside contact, she and her eight siblings did not know they were deprived.

Her life became brighter at nine years old when her father agreed to register her in school. Most girls did not attend school in the fifties and sixties. Or, if they did, they were already teenagers and did not stay long before they fell victim to the come-hither of young men, and on to marriages.

The school was a rectangular mud and thatch building divided into four rooms for classes one to four.

Njana's parents, like others, bought her a pencil and exercise books—one for writing and another with a multiplication table printed on the back and squares inside for arithmetic. Her class first learned how to say A-E-I-O-U and write ABCs and numbers.

From class one, the teacher wrote everything the pupils read on the blackboard. Since the school did not have enough reading books, the teacher read the book to the class. One book was about a clownish man called Abdullah, and another about *unjanja wa abunuwasi* (the tricky hare), the only two Kiswahili books Njana remembers through middle school.

When she and her classmates learned to read, *some*times the teacher passed the book around for each of them to read a sentence or a paragraph. Having previously read only words written in chalk on the blackboard, and mainly reading in unison, pupils initially were slow in reading from a book even though they knew most of the words.

They studied in Kiswahili and started learning English words when they reached class three. By class four, the teacher read, and at times translated, David Copperfield's *Oliver Twist* book to the pupils.

In class four—the highest level in the school—Njana looked forward to taking the national exam for the Certificate of Primary Education (CPE). This was the only path for a pupil to get admitted to class five in one of the few boarding schools in the country.

The majority of pupils did not attend school for more than four years. When they failed CPE, they started laboring alongside their parents on the farms. But a few repeated class four until they outgrew the class and the school terminated them. Njana dreamed of a better life and hoped to be one of the few exceptions.

But her boarding school aspirations had to wait because, although she was born healthy, unknown to her, her father was about to order her disabled for life.

*****

A month before the August school holidays, Njana overheard adults talking, lowering their voices if someone young went close. The one comment Njana recalls overhearing was that "children have reached the right age."

The right age? The right age for what? she wondered. What did it mean? She was determined to find out.

She soon learned from other children that it was about circumcision or "rites of passage," and that it involved cutting parts of someone's private parts. She winced, unable to contemplate why parents would allow such a thing to happen to their children.

She had not heard of or known anyone who had gone through initiation in the two villages where her family had lived. So she did not get overly concerned. She believed the people who had been confined in the native reserves during the Mau Mau war for independence had imported those strange practices to the British farms.

Those people did things differently from the ones who spent all their lives on the farms like Njana's family. They told unnerving ogre stories that would have got some authors drooling, itching to write that bestseller novel.

And unlike regular village women who hummed Christian songs, the Gikũyũland veterans sang rebellious freedom songs when they picked coffee cherries, harvested their employers' maize, or cleared land.

Because the colonial government had devastated the Mau Mau fighters— many of them hanged, captured, or surrendered before the end of the war— most villagers doubted the British would relinquish Kenya. Villagers said, behind the freedom singers' backs, that they were mere dreamers and wishful-thinkers. But the singers continued to sing in low, determined tones. They walked in measured steps and seemed prophetic and wise in a strange way.

Njana heard that her half-nephew Ngime and his female cousin Rembo, four months older than she, would go through the initiation.

Ngime was born in Gikūyūland but his parents had divorced, allegedly because his mother was "too lazy." He now lived with his uncle Kamau and family in Njana's village. Rembo, Kamau's daughter, had also lived in Gikūyūland during part of her formative years. The initiation rites that Ngime and Rembo found acceptable and even longed to undergo had nothing to do with Njana; she could not identify with them, she told herself.

Besides, her parents had been caught up in the religious wave sweeping through the villages and had become Christians.

Njana, however, could not claim Christianity; it sounded too alien and abstract. But, although she did not know what to believe and follow, she attended Sunday school and had assumed a Christian name ("Irene") two years prior.

Her religious sentiments failed to thrive when she started school and interacted with children from different villages. She realized she did not do things forbidden in the Ten Commandments. Why then did she need to pay attention to its mandates?

And as Njana progressed in school, she realized her family led a deprived life. She learned in Bible study that God had a "chosen people, the children of Israel."

Why would God choose some and not others? Did that mean God did not like her people? And the chosen people were not even Christians she was perplexed to learn.

Njana also failed to understand how her family lived in such squalor—despite her parents working too hard. Meantime, their employer worked little and lived in splendor, riding in motorcars. Why did God the all merciful not intervene? It confused Njana because the ones who prayed and praised the most seemed to suffer the most.

But when circumcision reared its head, and no other option seemed viable, Njana believed it was the one time Christianity would save her, not because of her own conviction, but that of her parents.

Njana already had role models. A couple of Christian families in the village had chosen not to circumcise their daughters who were older than she. Their fathers had evolved from such backward practices. But villagers termed the fathers' failure to cling to the rites of passage practice as "turning their backs on tradition."

What Njana did not know yet was that some Christians followed a hybrid religion—Christianity and their traditional religion. Her parents were of that type— parents who spoke all the words, did all the thinking, made all the decisions, and left little for their children as if they were mere incidentals.

Her father's word, similar to that of most other fathers in the village, was law in their household and no Christian rule was going to override his authority.

Njana sensed that her mother had tried to dissuade her father before she learned her fate. Perhaps the mother pushed him more than she had done on other occasions. But this is conjecture because no one told Njana. Maybe her father told her mother, and she, in turn, told Njana.

What Njana recalls is that while her mother was in her father's *thingira*, the designated man's house, she heard her father say in a tone of finality, "There won't be any uncircumcised girls in this family."

With that one pronouncement, her parents turned predators. Njana faced the biggest rift in her life, the rift that soon changed who she was created to be in this life. Her upcoming favorite month of August, with digging and gardening over for the year, and harvesting two months away, turned into a doomed month. Njana feared she faced a looming end of the world, her end of the world, as August neared.

Chapter Seven

The Waiting Game

Njana's agony progressed as August approached, wondering what part the circumciser would cut and how much it would hurt.

Two months remained before her fourteenth birthday, but all she knew at that time was that she used her vagina to pee. Having not gone through puberty or felt sexual sensations that, years later, she learned girls experienced, she had never felt a need to examine her private parts.

Now, unsure of the part of her vagina her father wanted cut off, Njana checked the sacrificial organ during each pee, wondering how she would look with part of it removed. How she hated to have an oppressive father like hers. How she envied her neighbors, Kesho and her sister, wishing she had a more modern progressive father like theirs.

She knew men and women did something, but what they did remained a mystery to her, just like where babies came from, two mysteries she had left well alone.

Now, Njana failed to understand why her father wanted to interfere with a part of her body that never bothered her. Surprisingly, instead of blaming her father for the decision, she hated the power adults had and exercised over children, from parents to teachers to nosy grownups on village pathways.

During the month-long wait, the villagers sang and danced on Friday and Saturday evenings. Njana had never seen Gikūyū grown men and women dance or sing in a group. Tugen—a pastoralist sub-group of the larger Kipsigis tribe—migrant workers were the only ones she had seen dance for pleasure during weekends.

Children never danced—it was supposed to be "unchristian." They sang at school only, standing erect as soldiers in a parade with only their mouths moving.

The circumcision songs and dances were different and robust. The singers celebrated the initiates, the tribe, and the Gikūyū enduring culture. They praised the candidates' bravery while their penises and vaginas shed their excess baggage. The singers used bad words and others Njana had never heard before.

Again, she noticed the only people who knew the songs were the ones who came to the farms from Gikũyũland.

Not knowing the actual date of the ceremony, Njana's anxiety and depression increased as August neared. She had never had even a hospital injection, so how was she going to tolerate a part of her body being cut off? She could run away, she thought, but no child had run away from his or her parents in Ilaso that she knew of. How could one do that?

At one time, she had heard that parents took their incorrigible children to live with their grandparents, but her siblings and she did not have a single grandparent where they could run for refuge—no need of wasting her thoughts on that.

Njana called for God's intervention multiple times. She could not visualize

God, but it did not matter—she evoked his name anyway. She said the Lord's Prayer, the only one she knew well.

The exercise failed to console her.

Usually, her mother's long prayer monologues bored her. But now Njana paid attention and listened to every word, believing it was more likely God the merciful would listen to her mother. But to her dismay, her mother did not include a plea for Njana's reprieve.

So Njana not only got bored by the monologues, she now loathed them, especially when her mother went on and on during meals. Meantime, Njana braced herself while her stomach growled and the food aroma became so enticing she could taste it. Why did her mother not pray before she ladled the food onto the plates? Njana wondered while she waited.

For those served first, there was always a child whose potato or whatever else found its way to the mouth before prayers began. Then the child averted his eyes like a thief on the lookout, straining to chew discreetly without making noises.

The only option left for Njana was to appeal to her mother—in her capacity as a Christian—to convince Njana's father to spare her. Perhaps her mother could approach him openly, in Njana's presence. This, she believed, would embarrass him and make him give in to the plea.

Njana's efforts went to waste. Without a confidant or cheerleader, she failed to garner enough courage and wisdom to construct a convincing story. Besides, the way her mother carried on, she seemed resigned to Njana's fate.

A tinge of doubt flashed through Njana's mind. Was her mother secretly in favor of the mutilation? It did not matter. Njana knew her father's ruling, no matter what her mother secretly believed, would settle the matter one way or the other.

Her mother, however, attempted to alleviate Njana's fears. She talked at length about the "symbolic" operation in Njana's hearing, no doubt for Njana's benefit. The audience was a woman who was visiting their house. Her mother spoke in a jovial mood, turning to Njana occasionally to ensure she was paying attention, as if it was just another family wrinkle to smoothen. The woman nodded and agreed with whatever Njana's mother said, no opinion of her own, but a mere sounding board.

Njana's mother claimed there was not much to the cutting. She explained how "superficial" the operation was in comparison with what she had had to endure. She said it was just a simple clitoral "nick," whereas, in her time, it was more extensive. She overlooked or did not want to elaborate on what "extensive" meant.

From that session, although Njana did not tell anyone, she realized her mother was not concerned about the mutilation, but about Njana's indecision and cowardice that needed to be overcome so she could be brave and persevere through the ordeal.

*****

Besides the motivational speech, Njana's mother did the best she knew to minimize her daughter's discomfort. She campaigned, she said, behind the scenes for Njana to undergo the initiation in private, which deviated from tradition.

Tradition called for the public to bear witness as a candidate crossed from childhood to adulthood.

Njana could only imagine how much her mother had debated with herself under such female powerlessness. That was if the mother did not harbor a secret wish in favor of the mutilation. Njana wanted to believe the former, that her mother was merely powerless.

Soon Njana learned of the "special" arrangement her mother had helped organize. Instead of joining about fifteen other candidates, her parents arranged a private ceremony where only two other girls would join Njana.

One of the girls had come from the city. Her body looked soft and smooth, an odd sight in those slave-labor villages. The girl also paraded about in shoes, an accessory the village girls did not have or miss yet. After she healed from the operation, she would return to her parents as if nothing had happened.

As an added bonus, Njana learned from her mother that the initiator would use a different razor for each of the girls. That was supposed to be progressive and special. But her mother never mentioned whether there would be any hand-cleaning before each cutting.

Her mother's assurances and efforts had not relieved Njana's fears and anxiety. But no matter how trapped Njana felt, she had to remind herself that it was not about her concerns and fears, her comfort, or her health. It was all about cultural adherence.

Days later Njana would find out cleanliness never crossed any one's mind. And why would it? Villagers were still ignorant about germs and infections, and most believed only the visible yucky stuff posed danger.

*****

During the eve of the event, a Friday, singers and dancers went to every courtyard that had an initiate. People celebrated the whole night. They had not gone to Njana's courtyard during the month-long festivities, perhaps fearing her parents, especially her mother, would send them away.

But Ngime, the half-nephew and one of the lead singers and dancers, seemed fearless, marching head-on to the target homestead. He led the group to Njana's full-moon-lit courtyard. She waited and waited for her parents to protest. Not a peep came from either of them. They did not even venture outside.

With her parents' implied approval, Njana planted herself on their porch to feast her eyes and ears. Her heart got excited when she watched the singers dash this way and that, urging the children of Gikūyū and Mūmbi to stand firm and not let anyone interfere with traditions dating back to Ndemi and Mathathi, centuries ago when the Gikūyū are supposed to have taken ownership of their lands.

The lyrics urged the initiates to march and brave the rites of passage like warriors headed to war and returning home victorious. The songs did tricks to Njana's soul and distracted her. She became an observer, watching and even enjoying the spectacle, if only for a few minutes at a time before she remembered she was the subject of the abhorrent practice.

After about two hours, under the songs' captivation and thoughts of the inevitable suppressed, Njana followed the group to another homestead before it ended at Kamau's compound—Ngime's uncle's homestead where most of the celebration had taken place.

Weary from staying too late and watching the robust group, Njana joined others inside the house. All the chairs were taken, so she stood, leaning against the center pole, her arm wrapped around it. To her regret, instead of resting, bothersome thoughts reinvaded her mind.

By then, she had gathered enough knowledge about rites of passage. She understood she needed to transition from childhood to womanhood. To do that, tradition expected her to soldier through the mutilation and not react to the pain. How was one able to face adult challenges if she or he could not handle a little cutting?

If an initiate cried out or screamed, she or he was labeled a coward, shunned, and treated as an outcast by the others.

When Njana learned of the stigma, she did not care. It sounded irrelevant as someone threatening her with old-age arthritis. She never socialized with any of the inductees before. Why would she want to start?

Right there and then, standing by that pole, Njana mused. If that kind of initiate's bravery was that important to the proponents of the mutilation, she would use it against her parents.

Meantime, Ngime took a break and entered the house where he noticed Njana. He approached her. He, a year older than she, eagerly awaited the circumcision, in a hurry to transition from a *kihii* to a grown man.

"Why a sullen face?" he asked Njana.

"I'm terrified of circumcision," Njana whispered. "I don't want it, but__"

"Are you going to remain a young girl forever?"

"How is that?"

"You need it to become a woman," Ngime whispered back.

"I don't want to be a woman."

"That's why you need it," Ngime said. "It'll help you avoid such foolish childish thoughts."

"I'll scream."

"What?"

"Yes, to get back at my parents for forcing me."

It was the first time, and the only time, Njana felt free to confide in someone.

Ngime chuckled, his hand over his mouth, while he looked from side to side as if to make sure no one else heard Njana. It soon dawned on her, with regret, that her confidence in Ngime was misplaced. Her woes were secondary to his goals.

Under the cover of poor lighting from two kerosene lanterns, Njana felt the first brush on the side of her thigh. A long but not fully grown penis alive, erect as a rod was on the prowl. Ngime started rubbing it on Njana's upper thigh and hip. He stopped after a few trials when Njana moved her body this and that to break the contact, and it seemed someone might notice their little dance.

That was Njana's first experience with a male primal sexual urge. Although she knew it was not proper, she could not figure out what Ngime wanted.

With no one else to confide in and discuss her fears, Njana's mind struggled, even at that late hour, to come up with a way to avoid the imminent operation. Perhaps if she struggled and screamed, the initiator might think she was too much trouble and abandon the mission. But Njana doubted that would work. If she struggled, it was likely the sponsor and the assistant would subdue her, and if they failed, the other women would help hold her down.

Maybe she could beg her mother to collude with the initiator whereby she would pretend to cut, maybe nick one thigh, but move on. She would get paid, and no one needed to know.

Njana did not approach her mother; perhaps she knew it was unlikely the scheme would work. Her mother might embark on another motivational speech to shoo away the cowardice. Or, if her mother went along, the initiator might not honor the agreement, believing she was doing an important job.

There was nothing left except for Njana to register her protest by screaming and embarrassing her parents.

Chapter Eight

The Initiator

Candidates were not supposed to see the initiator, although no one seemed to know the reason why, and those who knew, kept their lips sealed. The legend had it that the initiator sneaked like a thief at night, did her cutting, and disappeared.

Njana had no wish to see her hacker. She wished harm to the scrawny old hag she imagined. She hoped the initiator would meet with calamity to prevent her from getting to the village to accomplish her horrible and cruel mission. Njana's wish failed. As to who would do the evil deed was soon answered.

A person came under such a shroud of secrecy that Njana never learned when the person actually arrived at their home, perhaps before the family awoke. She only knew, no, she guessed, the presence from the way her parents guarded her father's *thingira.* They never allowed any child to enter.

The secrecy made Njana think the initiator possessed special powers. After all, rumormongers said she appeared on the day before the ceremony from a village whose name Njana never learned, and disappeared not a minute more after she completed her mission.

But Njana, without design, took a quick peek at the witch, nonetheless.

*****

Njana walked out of her mother's house headed to the barn. At the center of the courtyard she heard low voices to her left. She turned. Three women in a circle, bent from the waist, consulted each other and spoke in hushed tones at an area between her mother's house and her father's *thingira*, toward the back. One was her mother. Njana did not see the other woman's face, but the initiator stood out. She alone wore a multi-colored sheet over her dress, pinned or knotted over her shoulder.

Njana never recalls whether she saw the woman's face or whether the woman wore a headscarf like her two companions.

The initiator held an unfolded cloth in her hand. In it were several razors, which she was apparently showing to the other two women, hush-hush like a drug deal negotiation. She held out a black razor that looked like a tiny machete without a handle, about two inches long and an inch wide. The cutting-edge looked sharp and silvery.

Njana stood in the middle of the courtyard transfixed—from curiosity, fear, and awe. One of the women turned and noticed her and started to alert the others.

Njana dashed away.

Chapter Nine

The First Operation

On the doomed morning, nobody had to wake Njana; she had not slept. Well, maybe she did—perhaps for an hour. She went to bed at 3:00 a.m., not because she felt sleepy, despite her weary body, but her mother thought Njana needed sleep before her big day. But she stayed awake, wishing the night would go on and on.

In all her thirteen-plus years, Njana slept so well that a person could have broken into their house, carried her for miles, and deposited her in a different bed without waking her. But now she felt so anxious, she suffered from insomnia.

She awoke with a start from a nightmare of fighting to free herself from someone sitting on her stomach. The intruder had his or her back to Njana and was slicing her thighs with a carving knife.

*****

Just before dawn, a group of women marched the two victims and Njana to the Tinda River, about a mile from the village.

At the riverbank, the women helped the candidates take off their clothes, folded them, and handed each small bundle to a different woman—as if the three would not need them again. The lead woman instructed the three girls to get into the water while other women literally dragged them in.

"Squat! Squat!" they said in hurried tones. When Njana squatted, the ice-cold water reached to her chest. She shivered and grated her teeth. Her body bobbed out several times. She hesitated to cup her hands and throw the cold water over her shoulders to her back. The women would not put up with that. Two of them closed in—one held Njana down from the back to ensure she stayed submerged and the other scrubbed her down to her privates.

Njana later learned the bone-chilling water was the anesthesia, the numbing method the Gikūyū had used for hundreds of years. Much later, in her adult life, Njana learned that men also bathed in such chilling water to preserve and keep their testicles agile.

After about four shivering minutes in the water, the women hustled the girls out, instructed, and helped them to make fists with their thumbs snug between the index and middle fingers, elbows folded beside the body.

"Remain that way until I tell you to relax," the woman who helped Njana fold her fingers said. "If you feel pain, tighten the fists as hard as you can and focus on them."

The women made a circle around the three naked girls as a shield from view of any passerby early risers. They retraced their steps, scared, and shivering. Njana tightened her jaw to control her chattering teeth.

During their trip to the river and back, the women never talked amongst themselves or to the initiates unless they were giving instructions. Some women hummed while others nodded their heads in agreement, haunting bonding gestures about brave cultural troops going to battle and sure of victory.

Halfway, Njana's body disengaged. It had no feelings, the numbing coldness and nakedness forgotten. She became a mere observer, as if the process had nothing to do with her. She reengaged, ready to go through the motions only when they reached the scene of the crime.

*****

Njana's mother had a vegetable garden behind her house that extended about thirty feet before it reached the chain-link fence that surrounded the village. Her father had reinforced the fence with sticks so no one from the outside could see through to their homestead and the ones inside could not see beyond the fence. The mutilation "committee" had chosen the grassy area behind the fence as the perfect spot.

When the group arrived at the site, the women made an opening for the troops to pass through—then made a line and stood like sentries.

The girls' three sponsors sat in line, on stools about eight feet from each other, their backs to the fence, facing the line of sentries to the east. In front of each sponsor was a shorter rectangular stool for each of the initiates.

A woman helper stood by each sponsor. The three women came, held each of the girls by hand, and directed them to the low stools, each in front of her sponsor. Then, each helper went and stood behind a respective sponsor, to ensure no crazed candidate overpowered a sponsor.

Njana was first in line.

The minute she sat, her sponsor—Kezia—from behind raised her legs over Njana's folded knees and placed the legs inside, with her ankles level with Njana's instep. Kezia locked the two sets of legs in securely, and then pulled her legs apart. Njana felt as if any further pulling would split her in the middle. Kezia then wrapped her arms around Njana's chest. Njana felt squashed, without any ability to move, as if she were in a straitjacket.

From then, things happened swiftly.

The assistant behind her sponsor turned Njana's head to the left, facing the other two victims. "Stay that way," she commanded.

In seconds, Njana sensed someone in front of her. Her body reflexed, focus on her fists forgotten, when she felt hands by her thighs. Kezia tightened her arm restraints even more. Njana could not breathe. A pinch and a bolt of pain slashed through her vagina, traveled to her brain, and her whole body in a flash. She let out an air-piercing yell and followed it with two lower screams.

The helper quickly flipped Njana's head to the opposite direction, but not before her eyes caught a glimpse of a hurried stooped silhouette dash to the next victim, the city girl.

In the process of Kezia relaxing her legs to untangle Njana and the helper throwing a white sheet over Njana to cover her nakedness, the city girl had taken over the howling as if the two were in a relay. Njana never heard a peep after that. The third girl—the brave one—had to have tightened her fists, held her scream captive, and made her family proud.

With Njana's legs released and the white sheet fastened on her shoulder, the woman attendant produced some velvety leaves called *maigoya*, lined them like a pad, and she and Kezia covered Njana's deformed, traumatized vagina, then closed her legs.

The helper assisted Kezia to get Njana on her feet. She still suffered from slight shivers and felt dazed by the quickness of it all, unaware that seemingly simple act had changed the way she would from then on navigate the world as a woman.

With the mission accomplished, the initiator disappeared into thin air. Nobody spoke of her again. The group of women dispersed. Some returned to their homes and others went to Njana's parents' homestead to drink tea before they left. The old culture had won.

Kezia and her helper assisted Njana to make the slow, painful measured steps to the mud and thatch cottage where the city-girl and she would sleep on mats and call it their home for the next three weeks.

*****

The pain, mixed with the dream Njana had, made her believe the old witch had sliced the inside of her thighs. There was no way she could perform so fast with those clawed old hands without some extra nicking here and there.

The process was such a series of snappy choreographed steps that Njana thought there was no chance the initiator cut only the condemned body part, which, she learned a decade later, happened to be the center of a woman's sexuality.

Did the old woman even know to limit her cutting to what Njana's mother said? She did not know how the modern world lived, but at that very moment,

Njana knew what had just happened to her was downright wrong. But she also knew she had no recourse since her parents had turned predators. They were the final authority, especially her father.

That was what occupied her mind as she minced her lonely steps.

Chapter Ten

The Aftermath

Njana and the city girl settled in the small cottage where their sponsors returned twice that day to help them change pads. Afterward, Njana's sponsor, Kezia—24 years older than she and a divorced mother of three—remained and slept next door in Njana's mother's house.

The following day, Kezia taught Njana how to clean herself. After Kezia demonstrated the cleaning, she doused the wound with iodine from a small bottle that she left with Njana, and instructed her to use it daily after each cleaning. Njana did not have much to clean because after the first day the wound bled very little.

Kezia also warned Njana. If she did not clean and change the leaf pads often, Kezia said, her maimed organ's labia would fuse into one. That was the extent of Njana's education about the rites of passage.

Like the city girl, Kezia moved out of Njana's mother's house in three days. From then on, Njana slept and ate alone—with the occasional visit from her mother and sister. The two talked to Njana and made an effort to raise her spirits as if she were a patient.

Njana did not mind being alone. She spent that time thinking about her life, sometimes in bouts of long blank non-brain activity, a perfect meditation without intrusion from pesky thoughts.

When in thought, she dwelled on how much her life had changed for the worse in just one week. She wondered how to get used to her downgraded vagina, which she never paid attention to before, but now had to look at and attend to several times a day.

After she finished with the cleaning, before she installed fresh pads, Njana looked at her organ and longed for what could have been. Where did the cut part go? How big would it have become?

At a time like that, she longed for a long cleansing good cry. She tightened her eyes to get it going. Tears threatened all right, but not a drop dared roll out, each stunted, spooked, or congealed by Njana's troubled thoughts.

*****

Two weeks before the mutilation, the day Njana lost most of her hope, she had an accident at night. Unlike before when she dreamed of going to the toilet and waking up just before she started peeing, that time she peed and never woke up.

She had not wet her bed for years. But from that time on, she did it at least once a week, initially, before it diminished to only an occasional occurrence. It took her years of shame to re-train herself by avoiding liquids from late afternoon.

Besides the accident, the other main thing that Njana's mind dwelt on was education.

Before the culture warriors decided on mutilation, Njana had worried whether she would pass her class-four national exam, and join class five in one of a handful of public boarding schools. She wanted to attend Mang'u Girls, a Catholic school 130 miles away from her home. She had learned about the school through a family friend who attended the neighboring Mang'u Boys High School.

After the mutilation, she lost all hope. It was improbable the strict Catholic Sisters in Mang'u Girls would approve Njana's admission. She had heard reports that the Sisters examined girls and sent them home if someone had tampered with their private parts.

*****

After two weeks, the city-girl (the third, the brave one had joined the larger group) and Njana had healed enough to meet and go for daily walks. During one of their outings on the main dirt road that led outside the village, they bumped into the larger group of initiates—the braves—boys and girls. The two groups dressed in all white, like a teenage version of the terror group Ku-Klux Klan without the hoods.

The sight embarrassed and revolted Njana; it seemed the wrong image with which to identify. She already felt like an outcast and did not want to be one of those. Actually, she was not one of them. She had screamed. And, more than that, she had not quite accepted her new reality. She still fantasized about an uncut state. And her dream to pass the national test and attend a boarding school to become a learned woman remained intact.

Some teenage boys in the group taunted the two girls as cowards with tainted bodies. Njana fixed her eyes to the ground as she inched away. She and her companion never bumped into that group again. And, except for that one incident, no one mentioned Njana's shameful scream or the mutilation to her face, ever.

Yes, she was not one of them, Njana convinced herself; she would go on with her schooling. She clung to those thoughts as if that was all she had. Actually, that was all she had.

Otherwise she had nothing else clear in her life. She felt stuck, wondering how to respond when people started treating her as if she were a grown woman.

The hacking of her sexual organ supposedly had turned her into a woman. She tuned into her body but did not feel like a woman. How was she supposed to know how a woman felt like or how to behave?

She remained in that state of mind— wondering whether she had become a grown woman—well into her late twenties.

She wanted her life to remain the same as before, doing her chores, going to school, playing hopscotch, and jumping rope despite snickers that she was getting too big for such games.

Njana had yet to learn the gravity of how much circumcision had paved her way to a lifetime of sexual dysfunction. It had also turned her into a potential victim of rapists, gropers, and prowlers.

*****

Initially, Njana's mind played tricks on her. It is not too bad, she thought. Thank God it is the sixties; it could have been worse. So many women have gone through it. When she became a learned woman, she vowed she would move to a different place, where no one knew her past. Her secret would remain safe. She had no knowledge of gynecologic check-ups at the time.

Njana felt a tinge of shame and envy whenever she thought of or bumped into her neighbors, Kesho or her older sister. They were older than she and had not suffered mutilation. To her, it meant they were progressive whereas she belonged to a primitive era.

Commentary

Female Genital Mutilation is a milder form of castration, milder only because a woman can still procreate. It short-circuits the sexual system or dumbs down sexuality, at best. This may be similar to a violent rape, especially where a weapon is involved, only more devastating.

For rape, however, a woman can go through therapy and in time, with a good support system, she can have her impaired sexual and mental systems restored or repaired.

A mutilation victim, however, has had her organ—the epicenter of her sexual nerves—hacked away. This is physically, mentally, and psychologically damaging and permanent. Currently, therapy can help quiet the years of shame demons that reside in the heads of victims.

Reconstructive surgery is also available to a tiny fraction of victims who have access and the ability to pay. But surgery, like many other things in life, cannot correct a wrong. It can only lessen its effect.

Say, a logger cuts a tree down to half-an-inch from the ground. The farmer, the owner of the stump, complains the tree should not have been cut. Many years later, another sympathetic logger comes and promises to correct the wrong done to the farmer. He, the new logger, digs around the stump down another foot—does that bring back the whole tree?

*****

The best remedy for FGM has been education. Pushback or barrier against eliminating the practice has come from parents who remain ignorant of the harmful effects of FGM, and the people, especially the educated and the ones in power, who look the other way.

Chapter Eleven

A Taste of Adulthood

Njana's previous life of going to school, interacting with her family, and doing her chores had shifted, despite her resuming school in September as if nothing had happened during the August holidays.

Unknown to her, danger now lurked behind every village fence and shack's shadow during evenings. Meantime, she had to learn how to feel and use her newly acquired "young woman" status.

During December school holiday, she learned from her peers that she needed to exchange visits with other young women because, at fourteen, it was vital to make friends and learn to behave like an adult.

Shy and awkward, she had never made a friend besides the acquaintances she played or went to school with. Except on the eve of the initiation ceremony, she had never visited any other house in the evenings.

Njana started hanging out with other initiated girls, two of them much older and bigger than the rest. Over the next few months, one older girl who had never gone to school, dictated a couple of letters to Njana so she, the girl, could send them to her boyfriend.

Consequently, Njana took part in two evening social visits before she clammed up like a snail retreating to its shell, with no desire to venture outside after dusk. From then on, darkness or shadowy shrubs spooked her.

At Njana's first evening visit with several other girls, they ended up at the cottage of one of the bigger girl's boyfriend. Before they huddled together and slept, three in the bed she shared, that girl moaned and groaned, a few feet away. Njana later learned the girl and her boyfriend were having sex.

Early the next morning, Njana's slept-in dress was so wrinkled she felt embarrassed to face her family. She worried what to tell them. When she returned home, her mother paused from cooking morning porridge and shot Njana an evil eye but did not speak to her. Except to treat Njana as if she did not belong for a while, no one asked her where she spent the night.

Two weeks before the sleepover, Njana had already gone through her first sex education lesson, taught by the illiterate older girl, the only other girl who knew about boyfriends. Njana guessed the young woman was about seventeen or eighteen. Her family had come from Gikūyūland where she had gone through her initiation three years prior.

She taught three acquaintances and Njana adult sexual secrets that no one had the sense to teach them before.

She demonstrated by lying on her back. "A woman lies like this," she said, "and the man comes on top and puts his 'thing' in a woman's pee-pee. That's how women get babies."

It sounded gross to Njana.

"Do all women have to do that?" she asked, hoping there were exceptions.

"Yes, if they want to have children," the older girl said.

"I don't want to have children then," Njana replied.

"Why would a man put a baby inside a woman?" another girl asked.

"That's just how things are," the teacher said.

"I'll never get married," Njana said.

"How does the baby come out?" another girl asked.

"Through the pee-pee."

"You are lying," the girl said. "How can a whole baby come out of there?"

"I've never seen any baby come out of my mother," Njana said, shaking her head, more confused than ever. She thought the midwives brought a new baby to their house whenever her mother wanted one.

One girl was so flabbergasted that she watched open-eyed and never uttered a word. They finished the lesson with unsure giggles like little children.

That was the foundation of Njana's sex education.

Chapter Twelve

The Violation

Three teenage girls—Njana included—chatted and romped in the moonlight, close to the dirt road that led from the village. There was a half-moon, at about 8:00 p.m. In a village with no electricity, half-moon was a joyous time. A time to play and even chase fireflies, if the girls chose, without a nosy adult in sight to frown and claim they were playing like small children.

Four young men appeared at a distance. This did not concern the girls.

Everybody knew everybody in the village and people did not commit heinous crimes.

Villagers disagreed on offenses such as when boys fought or bullied each other while coming from school. Other quarrels arose from village gossip, or disagreeable drunks or when a neighbor appointed himself as the village moral enforcer and excessively disciplined his neighbors' children, mainly boys. Such incidents were always resolved among neighbors.

But these approaching four men seemed different. As they neared, the three girls recognized the voices of two locals who were in their twenties, but that did not make Njana feel safer. The men talked in low voices and stopped several times as if they were in deep negotiation planning a heist.

The girl who had moaned and groaned during the sleepover abandoned the other two. "Let me talk to them," she said as she skipped away. She joined the young men and even leaned her body against one of them—her moaning partner, Njana guessed.

Njana and her companion became uneasy, unsure what it all meant. "What do they want?" Njana asked.

"I don't know," the companion said.

It did not look good.

"Let's go home," they said, almost in unison.

After they walked thirty feet or so, they separated and headed toward their respective homes. The men said something about the two girls getting away. On hearing this, Njana and her colleague both broke into a run.

The next thing Njana heard was a pandemonium of hurried feet. One man said something to the other and then his feet ran toward Njana's companion. There remained two men. They headed toward Njana. The two started to argue as they gained on her. She heard their voices but did not recognize them.

As the men got closer, Njana panted so much she heard her heartbeat through her ears. She realized with horror that she could not outrun the two men. She was so focused on running and worrying, it never crossed her mind to scream.

She then heard one man threaten the other. "I'm not going to share," he said, "and I have a knife." One set of feet slowed; the other remained, gaining ground.

In another minute, Njana was yanked from behind and slammed to the ground. The man jumped on top of her, thrust his hands on her chest, and pinned her down.

The force disoriented Njana. In seconds her head cleared to realize her dire situation.

"Leave me alone! Leave me alone!" Njana said, as she pushed off her attacker.

The man fumbled with his trousers with a hurried right hand while his left forearm pressed hard on Njana's chest, endangering her ribcage.

In seconds, Njana's sex organ suffered another sharp whack, a second mutilation in months, the pain of which remains etched in her memory.

After the man got his quick thrill, he got up and hustled away, buttoning his trousers. Njana never saw a knife.

From that day on, Njana would relive that experience whenever she heard a woman claim, "He was my first."

When she stopped hearing the pounding of rapist's steps, she rose from the ground, straightened her crumpled dress, confused and ashamed of her life as she painfully walked home.

Three months prior, Njana had just turned fourteen, a small fourteen with breasts two years in the future. Her neighbors, Kesho and her sister, were much old than she. But since they were not mutilated, men did not bother them.

Commentary

Although FGM is now against the law in Kenya, there are still clandestine incidents, which are sometimes performed by medical personnel, and others not so clandestine, traditional style, practiced by some rural communities. Or when, on a rare occasion, a prominent person will dare to advocate returning to the practice as the news media reported that a female medical doctor did in January 2018.

Rape of teenage girls, however, has not declined. It has even increased in some poverty-stricken areas.

Mutilating girls' sexual parts is like a cult. The whys do not exist in the proponents' minds. It's hard to believe that the men and their henchwomen really pause and wonder why they support the grotesque practice.

Instead of protecting their young daughters, parents unwittingly become the main predators. They advocate, sanction, and facilitate the sexual assaults of their own children.

The practice of female circumcision, which is a euphemism for mutilating a woman's sexual organ, is centuries old. Reasons for the practice vary from place to place, but some communities don't even give a reason or discuss the practice openly.

When reasons are given to justify the barbaric practice, they include cleanliness, religion, tradition, and male domination. Except for the last reason, the advocates of the other three have given no plausible justification for their misguided beliefs or actions.

So the reason or reasons why the practice started and has survived this long have been lost in the annals of history. But it's not hard to deduce some of the present reasons when one looks at the populations that, among other oppressive behavior, adhere to and support female genital mutilation.

These societies also sanction or have sanctioned polygamy. In days gone by, it was usual to see men marry multiple wives—up to four in case of Muslims—but sometimes ten, twenty, or whatever number a man could afford to pay bride-price for as is the case of the Gikūyū people.

No matter what a sex machine such a husband was, no healthy wife would have waited sexually unattended for a year or two until she got ready to have the next child. But a gelded wife could stay put without much agitation until the *bull* made his rounds.

Besides control and domination of women through curbing their sex drive, mutilation also shielded child molesters and rapists (and still does to a lesser extent).

Occasionally, there will be a mention of westerners corrupting the morals of a certain society. The main moral mentioned is sexuality, from scant dressing to child molestation. This may be true, but before the westerners' infiltration, the claim goes that child molesters never existed.

The question to ask is would a man from a mutilating community molest a child if he could legally marry a nine-year-old, a ten-year-old, or a young teenage girl.

Again, parents, guardians or well-meaning defenders of societies do not go into the whys; they are on autopilot. *If it's in our culture, it has to be okay* kind of thinking.

PART THREE

Njana's story - 2

Chapter Thirteen

The Shame

People not familiar with mutilation and trauma suffered by sexual organs, and the aftermath of sexual disability, may not understand that the need for a victim to keep the experience hidden is a personal and lonely matter.

After all, many FGM victims come from areas where people have limited or no education or live in traditional, oppressive societies with little (or in spite of) exposure to the outside world. Parents are therefore adamant to retain their remaining, albeit many times watered down traditions.

Besides, many of these parents, including communities culture warriors, are ignorant of FGM's negative effects. Also, a segment of the civil society and the educated, who are in a better position to understand physical and psychological effects of FGM, merely look the other way; after all, they do not order their daughters mutilated.

In Njana's experience, the physical disability, as grotesque as it had been or may seem, was not as overwhelming as the psychological effect.

What years of torture. What years of shame. With whom could one share such private troubles? With therapists? No, many therapists in the West do not know the kind of man-created disability Njana is talking about.

She introduced the subject once to a health professional at an unusual medical challenges workshop in Hillcrest, San Diego. She wanted to know the different forms of FGM and their effects.

Njana raised her hand—easy when no one knew her identity. When she was called out and she asked her question, the speaker stumbled over her words and changed the subject.

From Njana's personal experience, she believes that anyone who had suffered any type of mutilation would never know or enjoy full sexual pleasure.

But, in her case, because of the several sexual assaults she had suffered in her early years, similar to lots of other poor girls in Kenya, it was hard to attribute the sexual malaise to FGM alone. Rape had to have played as big a part.

But, although she is not a doctor, Njana believes nature compensates for such deficiencies, like a brain creating new pathways.

An FGM sufferer might, therefore, enjoy sexual pleasure if the victim had a caring partner—especially if the woman did not know what she was missing. This could compare to a man and a woman finding ways to enjoy sexual pleasure even when the man suffers from erectile dysfunction.

Or does it?

Chapter Fourteen

Secret Anguish

On March 4, 2000, a couple of years after the unusual medical challenges workshop, Njana attended a book-signing at the Hall of Nations in the famous Balboa Park, San Diego's centerpiece. A young attorney of European extraction, who Njana presumed was the co-author, presented the book titled, *Do They Hear You When You Cry* by Fauziya Kassindja and Layli Miller Bashir.

Njana vowed to make a statement during the Q&A. But each time she gathered courage to raise her hand, her heart thumped, heat engulfed her body, and she felt as if something were stuck in her throat. The shame of declaring her secret in a hall full of people incapacitated her. Her sweaty hand remained on her lap; shame won.

After the presentation ended, people gathered in front by the lectern to talk to the speaker. Njana hovered behind. When the group dwindled to where no one remained close enough to hear her comment, she approached the young woman. She offered her opinion about the alleged *effects* of FGM—uncontrollable peeing, difficulty giving birth—that she believed the woman and other presenters had misrepresented.

Njana stated that the presenters had blown out of proportion FGM's medical complications without clarifying they were perhaps talking about infibulated[1] or re-infibulated women. Infibulation is the part that gets the majority of the press.

But if most FGM victims do not experience clinical medical complications, which they do not, then the proponents of FGM will believe their practice must be okay.

So to make the case for eliminating FGM, presenters and victims' advocates needed and need to give similar weight to the devastating sexual and psychological effects as well.

Perhaps they should even go further and let men know they would enjoy more and better sex from hornier, unmutilated partners.

---

[1] Excising the clitoris and labia and stitching together the edges of the vulva to prevent sexual intercourse

"Why didn't you speak up when everyone could benefit from what you are telling me?" the young woman asked.

Njana's brain froze. The woman had done a magnificent job in co-authoring the book, presenting, and advocating for her co-author's FGM escape and other women's traumas. But she had no clue of the difficulty and shame involved in a victim acknowledging and coming forward about such a painful personal issue.

Njana wished the woman knew the courage it took to approach her. Was it just academics for the young woman? Njana blamed it on her youth and inexperience, clasped her signed book to her chest with both hands, and walked out without another word.

*****

Njana's FGM thoughts came in bouts pricked by reading newspapers or watching TV. Otherwise, she relegated her concerns to the back of her mind until it came to her annual medical checkup and Pap smear—the peak of her shame.

Her discomfort started the minute she made an appointment to see a doctor as if the mutilation were the reason for the checkup.

She shunned female doctors, fearing they would compare her anatomy to theirs and heap pity on her. Or perhaps the mutilation would distract them and they lose focus on the checkup.

At one time, Njana felt relieved when someone referred her to a female doctor, originally from Haiti. She consulted the Haitian-American doctor for three to four years.

Every time Njana went to see the doctor, she ensured her anatomy was as clean as cleanliness itself.

One day, no matter how hard the doctor tried, she could not obtain a sample for a Pap smear test. She told Njana to make another appointment and "Don't wash that well next time."

That sounded patronizing to Njana. "Why didn't you tell me before?" she asked the doctor. "I clean like that whenever I come to see you."

"I thought it was your custom," the doctor said, looking at Njana with sympathy. "I didn't want to interfere with your culture."

Njana winced and felt worse inside. Who would have guessed that a learned woman of African descent harbored a down-on-Africa mentality? It pained Njana more because she expected the esteemed gynecologist, who had a spread on her hallway wall of photos of babies she had helped bring into the world, to impart such basics on Pap smear sample collection. And because Njana believed the doctor's "custom" and "culture" reference came from noticing her mutilation.

Afterward, Njana realized she had erroneously thought as a black woman, the doctor would understand her pain, advise, and chaperone her through the maze of women's health. Njana now knew, "understand" was a common burden people lay on black people as if they were guardians of world suffering.

Why then would Njana lay it on the woman? After all, no other doctor had ever advised her on the intricacies of her organ, let alone that her vagina was self-cleaning. And for whatever reason, it had never occurred to Njana to educate herself.

She had no knowledge, although she later learned, that deep cleaning might be detrimental to her health if it introduced germs or cleaned out the good germ-fighting bacteria.

Well, now that Njana's dream doctor had failed to turn out to be the health confidant she mapped out, she consulted mainly male doctors—they could not compare their anatomies to hers. She also changed them often so none could know her well. She wanted to remain incognito.

*****

The following is a replay of Njana's gynecological visits:

- Check at the clinic: complete forms, **wait**;
- Nurse takes blood pressure, pulse, temperature, height,

and weight (sometimes the last two overlooked), **wait**;

- Led to a cold examination room, change clothes—**wait**.

There is always the **wait**, maybe for "quality control"—to separate the sickest who cannot wait from the so-so sick.

When the doctor saunters in, he directs Njana to the display table; up her legs go, spread feet apart, heels into the stirrups. His hands clad in gloves, he leans forward, eyeballs wide and alert, to investigate and diagnose, or sometimes scoop a sample for a test.

The minute the doctor leans in, Njana shuts her eyes to steady herself, hoping she can meditate through the check-up. But she is the nosy type. She opens her eyes.

Just at that moment, she notices or imagines the doctor's jaw drop, a questioning, pitying look on his face. Did he blanch?

It's a quick flash, but before the doctor composes himself, the attending nurse notices. She throws him a quizzical look. But he's a pro. By then, surprise and pity have disappeared from his face.

The nurse settles back, confused. Njana guesses, the nurse concludes her boss is tired.

Composed, the doctor continues his investigation as if nothing is amiss. But he and Njana know the truth. His reaction hits her deep in her hurts' cave. She communicates with him in her mind, an explanation of sorts. Yes, I'm from those knuckleheads who trim their daughters' privates, Njana thinks.

Her mind tells her he throws her a look, then says, "I have heard of this, but I have never had a visual. Terrible practice! Awful!"

Njana eyes him. *You have no idea. I can't handle any pity or reprimand right now.*

A doctor's surprise or pitying reaction always pierced Njana's heart and nerve centers like a thrust from a thousand sharp needles. Her mind would then shift from the ongoing activity, concerned with how to override the pain and shame. *What is the doctor thinking? I wish I had not come.*

*****

Every time Njana went to see a gynecologist, she became anxious as if she had a dormant wound that flared the minute she made an appointment.

One doctor sneaked pitiful looks at her as if she were an infectious creature for him to fear. She could not handle such pity.

Njana stopped all gynecological medical check-ups.

Chapter Fifteen

Health Matters

Health was another challenge Njana wrangled with for a good number of years. She read a variety of books and magazines on good health and followed their teachings. She believed she could support her health through eating well and exercising.

Njana even plunged into fasting. She went for seven days without food except clear liquids, mainly water besides the daily glass of broth, and a clear glass each of fruit and vegetable juices. Hunger pangs disappeared in the third day. From then on, until she broke her fast, she felt the healthiest she had ever been.

After a three-year medical check-up abstinence, however, she became tired of TV guests' bombardments of eat this, don't eat that, you have to have yearly mammograms and pap smears, and walk-a-thon this or that. This triggered her doubtful thoughts, whether her methods of keeping well were disease-proof.

As if on cue, a troublesome infection developed that over-the-counter creams could not kill. The C-word terrified Njana. Cancer cells could be quietly munching on her insides.

She suppressed her shame and knocked on the doors of the medical community. She finally settled on a women's clinic in a not-so-trendy area, just east of downtown San Diego. She guessed those doctors must have come across every ailment and sexual deformity known to women.

At the 2-story run-of-the-mill clinic, they welcomed everyone who dropped-in—destitutes, uninsureds, and insureds alike. The big waiting room looked clean, with a reception room with a two-serve counter where patients checked in. Along two opposite walls ran a row of cushioned, dark-green plastic chairs. Another two rows of seats stood back-to-back in the middle of the room.

Women were the patients, but an occasional child, boyfriend, or husband tagged along.

When Njana phoned earlier, the receptionist told her she didn't need an appointment, although, with one, the wait time would be shorter.

It was an undercover mission for Njana—no one would recognize her in that part of the city. Besides, she did not intend to disclose her insurance, which meant no one would ever know, in case she had an embarrassing disease—a wishful thinking in record-keeping-crazed United States.

There were two lists at the counter: one for people with appointments, the other for walk-ins. Njana wrote her name on the walk-in list.

"Have you been here before?" the receptionist asked.

"No," she said. The receptionist handed Njana a stack of papers to complete.

"Njana!" the receptionist called out half an hour after Njana completed and returned the forms. "Do you have insurance?" she asked before Njana rested her arms on the counter while she leafed through the completed papers.

Njana waited until she leaned over the counter before she answered, "No—I mean yes! But I don't want to use my insurance."

"Why?"

How much is it?" Njana asked. She had put a dash in the income question space.

"It's on a sliding scale," she said. "How much do you make?"

Njana hesitated again, unsure of an appropriate way to avoid answering the question. Why does she need to know my income? Njana asked herself. And she speaks so loudly as if she's addressing the whole room.

"I asked how much you make!" the receptionist said as she looked up from the paperwork, snapped her head sideways to sweep her long black hair from her face, brow furrowed.

"Do I have to disclose my income?" Njana asked softly.

"Yes, or I can't help you. Everyone has to do it."

Njana cringed, imagining stares behind her back. "How much do I need to make to get the discount?"

"If you make $2,000 or more per month, you are not entitled."

"Okay, put down $2,000." Njana said. She wasn't eligible for government subsidy and, although she doubted she would be asked for proof, she did not want to chance it. Besides, she wanted to avoid anything that could be termed fraud.

"Take a seat; someone will call you."

Njana returned to her chair and resumed reading the book she brought with her. Except for an occasional child shrieking or running around, the waiting room had a relaxed atmosphere that helped her lose herself in her reading.

Two hours since she arrived, a nurse appeared and called her name from a door close to the counter; Njana hurried, glad to break the monotony of reading, dozing, thinking, and patients' watching.

At a station along the corridor, the nurse took Njana's vital signs—blood pressure, temperature, pulse, height, and weight. She then showed Njana into a doctor's cold office.

Njana did not wait long before a thirty-something, chubby white woman in a multicolored shirt top—like the ones worn by some kindergarten teachers—walked in.

Njana could not help but think—I waited all this time for a non-doctor? Would this woman know what ails me?

The woman introduced herself as a nurse practitioner. Not bad, but I want a real doctor, Njana thought.

"What can I do for you?" she asked.

"I need to see a gynecologist."

"We first need to determine that no one else can help you."

"Can I make an appointment to see the doctor?" Njana asked. "I don't mind coming back."

"You will go through the same process."

With no choice, Njana explained the infection, mistakenly expecting the nurse practitioner to give a diagnosis without taking a peek.

Not enough—the woman wanted to take a visual of Njana's privates.

"There is no need to look. It's exactly like I told you," Njana said, determined not to spread her legs.

"Do you know any African doctor you can go to?" the nurse asked.

Njana's thought process flipped. How did this woman expect a doctor from any country on the African continent to come to my rescue? Njana thought in quiet indignation.

In the absence of therapy, in spite of all the self-help books Njana had read, internal control had eluded her. She still harbored internalized anger that she had not tamed. She usually read between the lines in every statement. Sometimes that insight helped her guard herself from people who tripped her for just being herself. But other times it was uncalled for when she became defensive at a moment's notice.

"No, I don't know any doctor from Kenya," Njana said.

The woman threw her a look; perhaps she understood that Njana jabbed at her poor knowledge of geography.

Njana sat still, listening to useless words about benefits of a doctor from the same background. The nurse seemed unaware that citizens of the same country did not mean people belonged to the same tribe, let alone a whole continent.

Previously, when Njana explained that people could be from the same African country and be culturally different, it never seemed to register. So she did not bother to offer an explanation.

Done with her monologue, the nurse practitioner excused herself and left.

A different woman entered within minutes. She looked the part—a healing image—the signature white coat, perhaps in her late thirties or early forties. She looked Middle Eastern. Njana's body relaxed; this woman would understand. Njana had heard Middle Eastern tribes butchered their young women's privates mercilessly and she might not dwell on Njana's somewhat-lesser mutilation.

The woman turned out to be another nurse practitioner.

She started the same question routine. Njana repeated what she had told the kindergarten-shirt woman—about a stubborn "yeast infection." The nurse said there were several possibilities, but that she would have to examine Njana physically to eliminate them.

"But I'll run a urine test first," she hastily added.

Hmmm, no leg spreads for now. The kindergarten-shirt woman must have tattled on Njana. She left the clinic happy and full of hope.

But the urine test, and a few others done later, came out negative. Meantime, the infection raged on. Njana saw two other doctors; one of them gave her a one-time pill without examining her. The pill did not work.

Desperate, Njana went to Tijuana, Mexico, and had two more tests. The Mexican doctor seemed to understand the problem. He told her to stop worrying and gave her a tube of steroid cream. The infection cleared. But a week after she emptied the tube, the infection returned with a vengeance and even encroached on her buttocks.

Two years passed since Njana visited the run-of-the-mill clinic. At that stage, defeated, she just wanted to talk to somebody. She returned to her Middle Eastern nurse practitioner. Njana felt better when she communicated with her.

After Njana disclosed what she had been up to, the woman said, "Stop going to different doctors or taking medication. It might damage your liver."

"Really?"

"Really," she said and left the room. She returned with a tube of cream. "This is non-toxic; it'll soothe the problem areas."

The woman then said to give her a few minutes to think. She stood and walked about, deep in thought, stopping at intervals. "Excuse me," she said and walked out again.

Njana waited.

She returned, paper in hand. "I suspect I know what you're suffering from," she said. "But to be sure, I'll send you to a Planned Parenthood clinic. They encounter a lot of female issues." She handed Njana a list of clinics.

At the Planned Parenthood clinic in the Bankers Hill neighborhood, a woman dressed in regular clothes interviewed Njana. She never learned whether the woman was even a nurse. By then she did not mind whom she consulted, as long as they gave her hope of a cure.

Njana went over her problem one more time and answered the woman's follow-up questions. The woman excused herself and returned with a list of doctors' names. She put an asterisk beside one name. "Go see this doctor," she said, pointing. "She'll take care of you."

One more visit and a ten-year on-and-off suffering and mystery became resolved.

Psoriasis!

PART FOUR

Njana's story - 3

Chapter Sixteen

The Appointment

Sixteen years passed since Njana saw Geraldo Rivera and others talk about FGM surgery on TV. *Dear Abby,* the columnist, did not reply to her letter. If the reply appeared in the local newspaper, Njana missed it.

Now, she sat at home sorting papers when she came across the copy of that letter. She choked up when she reread the letter begging for help.

Despite her dread that somebody might see the letter, it had survived five moves. As she fingered it, she remembered how she had unsuccessfully searched on the internet—on and off for ten years—for a doctor who could perform FGM reconstructive surgery before she gave up.

In anguished despair, she tore the letter into bits, balled them, and thrust the ball into her wastebasket. But discarding the letter did not discard Njana's thoughts.

Days later, her mind remained stuck on a loop—if doctors could perform that specialized surgery in 1995, they surely could achieve better results with advanced technology in 2011. The thought energized Njana. She resumed her internet search.

A handful of doctors' names came up. One website showed a doctor with extensive experience in West Africa. Njana bookmarked the website. If she found no specialized surgeon closer to home, Njana planned to travel to West Africa.

Another doctor had an address in Colorado, United States. She browsed through her website and read the doctor's biography twice. It stated that Dr. Marci Bowers evolved from a physical man to a woman. Who would better understand her plight? Njana called the number.

"Yes, Dr. Bowers does FGM surgery," her assistant, Amy, said, "but the wait is six months to a year."

"A year?"

"She performs surgeries in clusters," Amy said. "She waits until there are enough patients to attend to in a day."

"No problem," Njana said. She was anxious to get on that list. After decades, even a two-year wait could not have fazed her.

*****

In January 2012, Njana drove on highway 5 North on her way to Los Angeles on a business trip. Just before she arrived, her phone rang. Good thing she had the forethought to wear an earpiece in case she received a call during her drive.

It was Amy from Dr. Bowers' clinic. Njana gasped, gripped the steering wheel tighter as her heartbeat quickened.

"Dr. Bowers has set a date for the surgery," Amy said.

"What?" Njana asked. After years of shame and private agony, the possibility felt so surreal.

"Yes, March 8th," Amy said. "Is this okay with you?"

"I'm ready tomorrow," Njana said and laughed to cover her nervousness and eagerness.

Amy chuckled. "I'll send you paperwork within the week," she said.

"There are tests that you need before surgery. Call me if you've any questions."

Njana was relieved when Amy said Dr. Bowers had opened a new clinic in San Mateo near San Francisco in Northern California. That was where she planned to perform the surgery. The appointment required Njana to consult with Dr. Bowers on March 7, one day before the surgery.

*****

The tests Dr. Bowers needed before the appointment included total blood count, EKG, and, worst of all, a written assessment by a gynecologist on the extent of the mutilation. Njana was free to choose the doctor.

She received satisfactory results of the medical tests one after the other. The mutilation assessment report read in part:

> "*She has slightly indurated introtus and reduced labia*

minora. She probably had stage 1 circumcision. She still has a small clitoris and clitoral hood, still has her labia majora, and the vagina is not a cloaca..."

The verbiage threw Njana off, but she knew "stage 1 circumcision...the small clitoris, and clitoral hood" had to be good.

This gave her hope. Perhaps FGM traumatized her more psychologically than physically.

Of all the times she disagreed with the "size doesn't matter" claim directed at men's privates, this was the one time she embraced the mantra without reservation, that "it's not the size, it's how you use it."

Chapter Seventeen

The Wait

Not in a position to know the extent or what her upcoming surgery entailed, the one and a half months' wait unnerved Njana. She became more emotional than she had anticipated. Some nights she slept no more than three to four hours.

She needed to talk about her secret with someone. But the thought of sharing with her friends made her cringe.

Since the mutilation decades ago, she had never talked about the incident with anyone, and no one, family or friends had ever mentioned it to her. That part of her life had remained hidden to the people she encountered throughout her adult life.

Njana was also involved in a difficult business deal that had no sign of getting resolved. To complicate matters even more, she had a new boyfriend she had not yet become intimate with. She could not bring up let alone confide in him about a problem that weighty and personal.

The only person she felt she needed to tell was one of her daughters staying with her at the time.

While the daughter watched TV, Njana asked whether she could talk to her. The daughter looked at Njana sideways as if to say; *get it over with so I can get back to my show*. It took Njana less than a minute to solicit the support.

"Good for you," the daughter said, quickly turned and resumed watching whatever she had been watching on TV. No reaction on learning her mother had been sexually mutilated, or a single question on when or where the operation would take place.

Njana felt so alone. Her thoughts sifted through her immediate network of friends and acquaintances in search of a person who could understand, care, and with whom she could feel comfortable discussing her upcoming big day. She phoned Thaka, a girlfriend who lived in a town near San Mateo, where the surgery was to take place. Njana had known her since class five. The friend had suffered similar mutilation, and Njana believed she was the safest person to tell and from whom to seek support.

She told her friend about the surgery and her dire need to share it with her two other close friends in San Diego. Thaka advised Njana against it. She also thought it unwise to have told the daughter.

No "good for you" or mention of her own mutilation escaped from Thaka's lips. Perhaps she did not want to be reminded of a subject she had "forgotten" decades ago.

Despite Thaka's coolness, Njana asked if she could recuperate in her apartment for a few days after surgery. Thaka paused for a long moment, clearly uninterested in rendering support. Finally, she said Njana to contact her closer to the surgery date.

When Njana called a week before she traveled to San Mateo, Thaka hesitated, then stumbled, fishing for words, the right words. She finally told Njana that she, Thaka, would be attending a meeting on that day. How about the following day? Njana wondered but did not ask.

Even if Thaka did not accommodate her, Njana expected her to ask for an update, then or later. To this day, although they talk often, Thaka has never asked Njana what happened. Perhaps she did not wanted to be reminded of her own ordeal.

During the mental turmoil, it never occurred to Njana to contact a therapist, which, in hindsight, was what she needed, a safe place to seek sympathy and pour her tortured overflowing emotions.

In another week, Njana could not bear the emotional pressure that weighed on her. She had problems focusing on her usual activities. She called and asked Amy at Dr. Bower's clinic to introduce her to the other three patients. Njana had already learned there were four of them.

Amy said she would email and ask the other participants, and then connect Njana with whoever agreed.

One woman chose to retain her privacy. The other two, Teta and Emine, originally from Liberia, then living in eastern USA, agreed to the introduction. Teta turned out to be single like Njana, but Emine was a wife and a mother. When they met later, the two women looked younger than Njana, possibly in their thirties.

The relief Njana felt when she connected with them was immeasurable, similar to what she had felt as a young girl when her mother returned home from a week's trip.

The three women supported and gave each other nourishing, impromptu therapies and assurances via email, texts, and phone calls.

*****

Njana booked herself a hotel room in San Mateo, a walking distance from Dr.

Bowers' clinic. She flew in on March 6, 2012, and planned to recuperate there for about a week.

The following day, she walked from her hotel, mainly for exercise, seven miles round trip to visit Teta and Emine at their hotel. They hugged, talked, and took pictures like old friends. Later that day, they met at the clinic on Bovet Road.

The clinic had scheduled Njana to consult with Dr. Bowers at 3:30 p.m. The time came and went. The doctor was still in surgery, the receptionist said.

At about 6:00, Teta and Emine went out of the building to stretch their legs. Since Njana had just been outside, she remained in the waiting room, seated across a coffee table from a young woman. She was tall, skinny with shoulder-length hair, light-skinned—the type marketers favor to model at upscale establishments.

The receptionist busied herself at the counter, yards away.

"I doubt Dr. Bowers will make it this evening," Njana said, just to make conversation.

"She's coming," Miss Model said. "She called when you were outside." She then buried her face back in the magazine she held in her hands. She and Njana never exchanged another word.

This woman cannot be here for surgery, Njana thought. She is too young.

Tired of her own company, Njana joined her two colleagues outside. One of them said Miss Model was one of them, the fourth candidate who did not want to be identified. Njana doubted it.

In the late twentieth century, most FGM practice had been phased out, or the holdouts had mostly gone underground, at least in Kenya. The ones who still practiced it lived in the backwoods, determined to hold on to their old traditions.

Miss Model with her flawless skin seemed city-bred. Perhaps Njana did not want to imagine one that young and beautiful had undergone such a heinous life-changing experience.

*****

At about 7:00 p.m., the receptionist announced Dr. Bowers' arrival. The women hushed and shifted in their seats, ready to meet their Redeemer.

The receptionist ushered them in, one by one. They behaved anxiously, although far less so than during the mutilation, at least for Njana. This time, however, they were willing and eager to get poked and rearranged.

Njana could not wait to meet Dr. Bowers. When her turn came, the nurse led her to a typical doctor's examination room. It contained a bed, a stool for the doctor, a chair for the patient, a sink and medical paraphernalia. Njana felt at home right away. Dr. Bowers followed typical doctors' protocol:

- Overlap patients' appointments and keep them waiting—check
- Stock germy magazines—check
- Make sure the examination room is cold—check
- When the doctor finally appears, he or she asks two questions and makes a split-second mental note of the diagnosis, followed by a two or three minutes'—five, tops—checkup to confirm the already pegged diagnosis.

For Dr. Bowers, Njana had to wait and see.

That March 7, however, she did not mind the wait.

Chapter Eighteen

The Second Operation

While Njana waited patiently, drank with suspense, in the examination room, her mind wondered what Dr. Bowers could possibly do. Short of a transplant—an idea she had kicked around in her mind before—what else was there. The doctor's entrance interrupted her train of thought.

Dr. Bowers wore the signature white coat, a real doctor's coat. Tall—six feet?—and skinny, perhaps in her forties, with flowing blonde hair down to her shoulders, some of it clipped behind her head. Her face looked fatigued, but she approached

Njana where she sat on a chair, her hands in her lap, as if she were her first patient of the day.

She and Njana engaged in get-to-know-you pleasantries.

Commentary

Initial pleasantries with a doctor are always iffy.

"Good morning," a doctor says, or "Good afternoon."

"It's not good." Is that what a patient should answer?

How about, "How are you?"

Should the patient say, "Sick," groan or assume a pitiful face and dive into his or her bodily aches and pains?

*****

Dr. Bowers pulled her seat diagonal to Njana's, next to the examination table. She put her hand on one of Njana's. A healing soft hand—the softest cool hand Njana had ever encountered. The doctor's calming words of encouragement soothed Njana's fears. No doctor had ever displayed such concern and addressed her with care, without words or face crowded by haste.

When the doctor said she needed to *look*, Njana hung her legs into the usually scary stirrups without a care. She did not mind Dr. Bowers pulling her soon-to-be-assaulted body part from side-to-side and upward, still curious and doubtful of what the doctor could do.

"What do you think? Njana asked, "Any hope for me?"

"You are a good candidate," the doctor said. "You will be quite happy with the results."

"You really think so?" Njana wanted to believe the doctor and clear all her doubts.

"Yes, the cut was only superficial," Dr. Bowers said, "most of the clitoris is underneath and that is what the surgery helps to bring to the fore. I construct it as close as possible to its original state."

*****

The following morning, March 8, 2012, Njana arrived at the clinic at 7:00. By 9:00, nurses wheeled Teta, one of the two Liberian women, toward the recovery room while she talked incoherently but at times clearly about fearing somebody would hurt her dog.

In their interaction the previous month, she had never mentioned a dog. A tinge of fear hit Njana. She wondered what nonsense or secrets she would reveal under the spell of anesthesia.

Njana waited in the room adjacent to the operating room (OR), at the western side of the building. A nurse had already prepared her for theatre—robe, cap, and fluffy slippers. Miss Model walked in, wearing similar theatre garb. She walked in measured steps, a nurse beside her. The nurse helped her sit in one corner.

Njana stealthily eyed Miss Model as she leaned forward lethargically, eyes to the floor, likely after having received an injection of mellowing meds.

The nurses, in typical fashion, did not heed privacy concerns. One of them told Miss Model loudly, "Your husband will wait in the outer room until after surgery."

Njana suppressed her plight for a minute and thought how pitiful for such a young beautiful woman to have been sexually damaged. Well, at least, she has a husband waiting and rooting for her, Njana thought, whereas I have to sneak behind my friends.

*****

Since the session with Dr. Bowers the previous night, Njana's emotions had settled somewhat. Her mature veins, however, were another matter—they remained spooked. The nurse could not find a prominent vein on the back of Njana's hand, where she needed to insert a humongous needle through which the anesthesiologist would later feed the required poisons into Njana's body.

The clinic had turned down Njana's request for a local anesthesia, the reason why the nurse had poked her hand for the umpteenth time. The nurse needed to stop the prodding, do it better, or summon reinforcements.

A black woman came to check the reason for the delay. The poker stammered and her hand became unsteady. One more poke and the nurse could not bear the gaze of a vigilant witness. She dashed off and soon returned with another nurse in tow, perhaps one with more experienced hands, Njana hoped.

The newcomer coaxed a vein in seconds. She then injected Njana with a dose of poison—to make her "comfortable," the nurse said.

She had told the truth. After that, Njana's mind became euphoric. She did not care what they did to her—poke, cut, or feed poisons into her veins.

When nurses wheeled her into the OR, Njana observed, or sensed, a lot of activity around her. In another minute she was hoisted like an invalid onto the operating table, the typical huge surgical light hovering above her. The black woman came and stood on one side of the table. She talked to Njana as if she were a VIP.

"I'm Diane," she said. "I'll keep you comfortable while Dr. Bowers takes care of you. I'm the anesthesiologist."

Dr. Bowers appeared and stood on the other side of the table, across from Diane. She engaged Njana in some small talk. Meantime, a male doctor came and stood at the foot of the table. Dr. Bowers introduced Dr. Jackson and said he was the observer. Njana had given her consent for Dr. Jackson to observe when Amy told her that the doctor planned to go to perform clitoral restorative surgery in West Africa.

The three individuals looked down where Njana lay, but she never felt any anxiety. Dr. Bower's clinic adhered to racial diversity. So far, the receptionist and the nurses Njana had encountered were brown; Diane (Njana never learned her last name), the anesthesiologist, was black, and the two doctors were white.

As Njana's team engaged in trivial talk, possibly to distract her, Diane placed a needle into the receptacle that the nurse had taped almost permanently onto the back of Njana's hand. Diane started pumping a syringe full of poisons as she said, "I'll get this in slowly. You won't feel anythi...." and then everything went blank.

*****

Njana moved her head from side to side like an infant, not able to hold it up. Her body had no other feelings. Then she became aware of a barrage of noises and shakes on her upper body. All she wanted was to fade away and sleep, but the noises and shakes would not cease. She tried to protest, tell the cause of the disturbance to leave her alone, but her mouth refused to cooperate

The noises became voices. But Njana could not make out the words—her brain was on strike. She saw a flash or sensed images. Yes, there were two blurry images, perhaps from the shakers, one on each side of her bed.

"Njana! Wake up! Wake up!"

She wanted them to stop shouting and shaking her shoulders. She felt so tired. She just wanted to sleep.

These are women's voices—where am I? she wondered. The images gradually came into focus. Two animated women bent over her. Their chatter disturbed her.

Why can't they stop talking? Njana thought.

In between the shakes, the women moved her. Her brain started to come alive. She realized she was now seated on a bed, slouched.

One of the women brought a glass to Njana's lips. She ordered her to drink. Njana took a sip or two of the liquid.

The women's voices became clearer.

"What a relief!" one of them said.

Nothing made sense. But somehow Njana remembered, just a minute ago, a woman was talking to her. What was her name? That was in the OR. But she was not there anymore. Her bed was now curtained off except the footboard side. The two busybodies were nurses, Njana could tell from their green or blue uniform. Her body felt lethargic, but her thinking returned.

"How long have I been here?" she asked.

"Too long," one nurse said.

"How long?" Njana repeated.

"Two hours longer than expected," the other nurse said.

That explained the commotion, and the reason they kept checking Njana's blood pressure. After the nurses realized Njana was aware of her surroundings and fully awake, they held her up from her armpits and walked her to a chair. They smiled and agreed the worst was over.

"Yes," Njana agreed, although she had no perception of the danger in which she must have been. She did not feel any pain or any awareness of the bundle between her legs. But, gauging from everyone's celebratory reaction in the recovery room and nearby, Njana realized she had spooked them all. They must have feared she survived FGM as a teenager, only to succumb to it in her golden years.

Drs. Bowers and Jackson appeared, still in their theatre scrubs to converse with Njana. She was still in theatre gown herself. Njana said it was a historic moment, stood, and asked a nurse to take a picture of her with Dr. Bowers, and another of the two doctors.

Afterward, nurses helped Njana change into her clothes and sent her to the hotel in a taxi in company of a nurse.

Another nurse came at dusk, kept an eye, and tended to Njana most of the night. The first few hours were critical because of possible excessive bleeding. At about 2:00 a.m. the bleeding subsided and Njana wanted to catch a snooze without the nurse's "How do you feel?" and "Can I check?" interruptions. She then insisted it was okay for the nurse to leave.

*****

Just days after Njana returned to San Diego, she was touched when Diane, the anesthesiologist, phoned to check on her progress.

By the end of the prescribed six-weeks healing period, the mutilation scar was no longer visible.

Njana, Tate, and Emine kept in touch. They compared notes while they recuperated, each happy with her results.

PART FIVE

When sex becomes a chore

Chapter Nineteen

The Golden Years

Mume crawls cautiously into our bed as if he does not want to wake me. As soon as he settles in, his hand starts feeling me here and there. I don't flinch—maybe I do, a little, but I don't let on—hoping he will believe I'm in deep sleep and abort his urges.

But his hand continues its journey around my body, traveling south. In our high tide era, the hand used to start north and progressed downward. It never starts or goes north anymore, at least since after the children.

I touch you knowing we weren't born tomorrow
And somehow each of us will help the other live[2]

My mind wonders. Are the two of us just helping each other live? How should I react? I have brought forth and raised four children, and now have six grandchildren. Oh, the joys of having little feet pattering around the house on weekends. They represent one of the major joys of my life.

I feed their grandfather his favorite meals—most times—wash his clothes, and keep the house sparkling clean. It's not that I do the actual cleaning—I have a woman who helps with that—but I manage and organize the family house and affairs.

I also accompany my husband to an occasional event; mainly the ones he chooses—even if some of them bore me to discreet nods—partly to prove he's happily

---

[2] From Twenty-One Love Poems (Poem III by Adrienne Rich)

married. The image of looking successful and happy is important to him. I welcome such image, too.

I have given much to this marriage. But given our last two years' experience Mume should stop recycling our past bedroom romps—age frowns on do-overs.

I'm done.

If he gets sick, however, I'll be in the middle of his healing—companionship and emotional support, too. But any bedroom activity beyond sleeping? No. I need to put a stop to it right now. If I don't, he may never believe I really need him to stop.

"Um!" I say and thrust my elbow toward him. It barely taps him. It's not as if I'm trying to hurt the man; I care for him. I just want him to keep his hands to himself and let me enjoy the rest of my bedroom life in peace.

"Mume, aren't you embarrassed to touch me like that?" I say, in case the elbow fails to convince him. I wait for my words to take effect, my sleep pretense on hold.

"S-i-k-u," Mume says, so softly I can barely hear him amidst his engaged, heavy breathing. That always gets to me—when he stretches my name sweetly like that. But the hand halts, jarred, waiting for the master to give further orders.

I pause. Both of us pause, the hand and I.

"We are too old for that business," I say, exaggerating my grumpy, half-sleepy voice, determined not to get sucked in.

The hand pulls back slowly, away from me. Without another word, Mume turns his back to me.

I feel a twinge of guilt, a has-been wife. I take a long time to entertain sleep.

Instead, I get stuck on my thoughts, the uselessness of the occasional starving to which I have subjected myself. I have avoided those hip-packing chips I love to munch on, determined to maintain a body my husband can admire and wrap his arms around.

But I cannot take all the credit for the trim body I flaunt around fellow senior citizens who ogle me with envy.

"What do you do?" I hear from an envious voice on occasion.

"Nothing," I say. "It's my genetics," I add, thankful the busybody does not know any of my waddling relatives who store food in their bodies instead of in granaries.

Actually, part of the credit should go to the woman I bumped into over a year ago.

"I haven't seen you for months," she piped. "When are we eating njahi?" (the white-eyed peas cooked for new mothers) all the while her eyes fixed to my stomach. An acquaintance, no less; I could have smacked her. The nerve!

That very day, I rushed home as if a stalker was on my heels. I trashed all the household junk that masqueraded as snacks; munching them as if I were a goat being fattened for slaughter.

No more.

In one year, I strutted with the best of them—seniors, I mean. But even with all that labor, the bedroom activity remained sluggish.

I now wonder when age took over and snuffed out the intense physical longing we two, Mume and Siku, had shared.

It's not as if I dislike his closeness. I enjoy when he occasionally slows down, we kick back, talk shop, and enjoy a drink. I especially love the follow-up cuddle when sleep overloads my eyes while I'm in his arms.

But for Mume, a cuddle still seems to be a sort of prologue to a bigger and better activity while I'm already teetering on a relaxed conclusion. As much as I love to cuddle, it's now on hold.

*****

For more than two years, whenever we are in bed and his urges hit, my mind races in many directions, including how tired I feel. I have updated Mume on the state of my body, hoping he would take a hint and quit altogether. My prods have not worked.

Our intimate relationship has not fizzled. It's comatose. He seems not to appreciate that I'm an older woman, and most of my estrogen is depleted, kaput.

At the beginning of the downward slide, like a caring wife, when my body displayed unmistakable effects of estrogen erosion, like dryness and heat-wave menopause, I went along with his sexual appetite. Considering his age (he hates when I mention age in the bedroom), I secretly wondered whether his stamina was Viagra-induced.

Whatever the case, my experience felt like a pump and dump. (Sorry for the crude term. Nasty language grates my mind as well, but I don't have a better substitute right now.) After too much of that, I had had enough pretense.

Now I wonder whether he recalls when I yelped in pain; perhaps he does. He introduced the cream soon after. Said it would help our conjugal relations. When the cream did not work its magic on me, I kept mum. But Mume knew. He saw through my pretense. There was no hiding my body from him. The years we have been together, he has explored around the tiniest nerve, flab, and curve that could spark a sensation.

Yes, the cream did not do much for me. I never cared for it. But, for Mume's sake, I made an effort. I really did, like a good, caring wife should. But our bedroom activities remained bland. Not a single sensation teased my nerves. Nothing. That concerned and embarrassed me for him.

In all that time, I never suggested anything. In my frustration, sleeping in separate bedrooms bounced into my thoughts, but I kept it to myself.

Just before Mume and I gave up on the cream, he came up with the next sure-thing—hormonal replacement therapy.

Oh my, two different remedies back-to-back? Can I have a break in-between? That was all I could think.

There was no way I was going to dab on that *sure thing* either. Not when cancer is peppered along my bloodline, as deep as neurons and synapses can nudge my memory. At the time, Mume resorted to his S-i-k-u. I told him to weigh cancer and sex. What could he say about that?

Nothing.

There was no point of us reliving our lives; that's what I said.

*****

Now, since Mume has withdrawn his hand and stopped begging any more, while my brain goes on a safari[3]—the highs and lows—of our bedroom activities, my mind

---

[3] Kiswahili word for tour, trip, or journey

calms. I sleep for four hours straight. But the minute I stir, my mind jumps back to our marriage. To shake it off, I plod to the kitchen and drink a glass of water. Back in bed, my mind spins.

Does Mume wonder why I kept mum when he strayed? Does he think I didn't know? What did the young woman see in him? Perhaps an outing, a good meal, and a gift here and there by a man in a suit made her think he was rich. Or maybe he toyed with the d-word, promised her he intended to divorce me.

For his sake and hers, I hope Miss Young did not believe his wild stories when she stuck around for over a year. The truth is I don't care what he told her. He is my family and belongs to our home. He is here to stay simply because he is settled in and set in his ways. And he is not irresponsible or stupid to bring forth another child, although our marriage can withstand any tsunami. I harbor a deep knowing that a sneaky death is the only bugaboo that will draw a line between us—Mume and me.

Besides, Mume, well, we don't have enough money to share, and he is too scared I might decide to get nasty and force a fifty-fifty split and kick him from the nest, an act that makes men's insides quake.

That's the reason I want him to let me be. The minute he makes a move, my mind makes flips and weaves through all that history.

Back then, I resisted telling him the other reason that made me bail out of bedroom antics sooner than I should have. I feared it would hurt his feelings if I told him that he took me for granted. Maybe I take him for granted, too.

Like many men, he mainly focused on the grand finale. No clue on what makes a woman follow a man as if he has sprinkled a captivating scent in his wake. It's the *verbal communication*, frivolous or not, coupled with caring and a *soft gentle touch*.

Mume also did not appreciate that sex ebbs when babies come along or a woman gets on in years. Of course, there is always an exception, but I'm not talking about the outliers. I'm talking about older women like me. We are the norm.

Mume wanting a romp did not mean I was ready or receptive, no matter how much the media touted the drivel that "sex gets better with age."

I have to stop rehashing all this and get back to sleep.

YEARS of SHAME

Epilogue

When raising Binti, the daughter born at the women's factory, Njoki may have confided in a friend or friends that Binti was an Oops! child and, even worse, that she turned out to be a girl. Binti had to have overheard those rumors. In her teens, as she blossomed into a potential head-turner, but unaware of the inherent benefits of beauty, she fought with her mother as if the two were on a battlefield.

"It pains you that I'm the last born," Binti would tell her mother after the two exhausted themselves going at each other. "You wanted my brother to remain the last born. Now, you have to deal with me."

In her twenties, Binti remained belligerent, never slowing her vile behavior toward her mother. Finally, she showed total indifference even when the mother's body, weary of disease, lumbered along for two years before it succumbed.

Afterward, with only one parent left, Binti dilly-dallied through her life, but in her thirties, the gossip she may have heard did not serve her anymore, especially without an opponent. She buried the matter and embraced life.

She is now happily married with two sons.

*****

As for Njana, because of the way she sneaked around, trying to conceal her condition from her boyfriend, he believed she was trying to settle a previous relationship. Tired of his questions and his attempt to get intimate, she told him about the reconstructive surgery after three weeks.

"We'll just have to deal with it," he said.

Njana's main benefit from the surgery was psychological. When she made the next appointment for her annual checkup, she did not fret or connect it to her previous condition.

As for the rape Njana suffered at fourteen, she disclosed, with trepidation, the decades-old incident for the first time during the interview for this book. Even then, she wanted to remain anonymous.

*****

The story of The Golden Years is included here because there comes a time when women have to do what they feel comfortable with irrespective of who gets disadvantaged in the process.

The last story is based on two incidents—one is about a husband in

Nairobi who shared his marriage concerns with the author's cousin. The second incident is of a husband in San Diego who aired his frustration with the author.

In both of these cases, the husbands had complained that their wives had turned their backs on bedroom activities.

The San Diego husband had recommended remedies, but his wife became tired of the hassle, worried she might get cancer while trying to keep her husband happy. She told him, "We don't need sex at our age," the husband shared with the author. They were in their sixties at the time.

The Nairobi husband did not know to suggest any remedies. Sexual props are not widely accepted there. According to him, when he closed in and touched his wife suggestively, she said, "Aren't you embarrassed to touch me like that at my age?" He had recoiled and kept to himself, he said, no doubt to find solace elsewhere.

Except for the quotes, the author has merged the two wives' stories and filled in some blanks.

In accepting their reality, both husbands joined hordes of other husbands who shun or are not interested in the d-word; these husbands prefer settled, family lives. So, they set-up mistresses, sneak a one-nighter now and then, incorporate their exercise regimen with an occasional dash to a discreet massage parlor, or pick up women of ill repute.

The two wives embraced ignorance and carried on as if their bedroom lives were as they had always been. The good thing is each of the four individuals got what he or she wanted, or close to it.

If you enjoyed reading this book, please leave me

a review on **Amazon.com**

https://t.co/lIjX2TO9b3

Wanjiru Warama

Acknowledgments

My thanks go to the following people for their support, feedback, and suggestions. They include Janet Hafner, Mary Kelley, Kathy Davis, Jeanne Rawdin, and Dave Fymbio for the cover design.

And I thank you for your time in reading the book and making it all worth it.

Wanjiru Warama

The next book

The next book will be set in Kenya when Ms. Warama's parents scratched a living on a farm owned by a British farmer.

The book will show how colonization and subsequent Mau Mau war of liberation affected and shaped the author's life and that of her family.

For future updates sign in at her website:

wanjiruwarama.com

(Under contact)

Author Wanjiru Warama writes books that entertain and inform. She was born and raised in Kenya when the country was a British colony. She now lives in San Diego, California.

Visit her website: wanjiruwarama.com